TWIST & SPRITZ

Published by Parragon, Ltd.

Photography by Mike Cooper and Günter Beer
Additional photos used under license from Shutterstock.com

ISBN 979-8-89019-176-2

NOTES FOR THE READER

This book uses standard kitchen measuring spoons and cups. All spoon and cup measurements are level unless otherwise indicated. Unless otherwise stated, milk is assumed to be whole, eggs are large, individual vegetables are medium, and pepper is freshly ground black pepper. Unless otherwise stated, all root vegetables should be peeled prior to using. People with nut allergies should be aware that some of the prepared ingredients used in the recipes in this book may contain nuts. Garnishes, decorations, and serving suggestions are all optional and not necessarily included in the recipe ingredients or method. The times given are only an approximate guide. Preparation times differ according to the techniques used by different people and the cooking times may also vary from those given. Optional ingredients, variations, or serving suggestions have not been included in the time calculations. Please consume alcohol responsibly.

TWIST & SPRITZ

PARRAGON™

CONTENTS

INTRODUCTION

THERE'S SOMETHING IN THE AIR during summertime, a sense of joy and levity. An ease of living. Slowing down and appreciating quality time with family, friends, and oneself. And there's no denying that a cocktail is the perfect complement to appreciating summer and all its magic—a good meal among loved ones, time spent on a pool deck, or relaxing in a comfy chair after a long day in the sun. Few things say "enjoy summer" like sipping a spritz cocktail.

Originating in northern Italy in the 1800s, the spritz cocktail was created when people wanted to make wine that they felt was too strong a little lighter by adding a splash of water. Soon flat water became soda water, then sparkling wines and liqueurs were introduced.

To honor its origins, you can enjoy cocktails that feature Italian flavors, like the Limoncello Spritz (page 39) and the Negroni Spritz (page 43). You'll also find sparkling punches and large-batch cocktails that are great additions to summer parties, as well as traditional aperitifs and classic spritzes, like the Hugo Spritz (page 19) and the most famous spritz of all: the Aperol Spritz (page 16).

In this book is a collection of spritz cocktails perfect for celebrating and delighting in everything good that life has to offer.

GLASSWARE

PRESENTATION IS EVERYTHING in mixology, so it is important to serve a cocktail in the appropriate glass—the size, shape, and style all have an impact on the visual perception and enjoyment of the drink. Here are some of the classic glasses you will need to have in your collection.

MARTINI GLASS

As the most iconic of all cocktail glasses, the conical glass emerged with the art deco movement. The long stem is perfect for chilled drinks, because it keeps people's hands from inadvertently warming the cocktail.

HIGHBALL GLASS

Sometimes known as a Collins glass, these glasses are perfect for serving drinks with a high proportion of mixer to alcohol. The highball glass is versatile enough to be a substitute for the similarly shaped, but slightly larger, Collins glass.

OLD-FASHIONED GLASS

The lowball glass, also known as a rocks glass, is a short, squat tumbler that is great for serving any alcohol on the rocks, or for short, mixed cocktails.

CHAMPAGNE FLUTE

The tall, thin flute's tapered design reduces the champagne's surface area which helps to keep the fizz in the drink for longer. The flute has now largely replaced the coupe glass for serving champagne and champagne cocktails.

SHOT GLASS

This glass is a home bar essential and can hold just enough alcohol to be drunk in one mouthful. It also has a firm base that can be satisfyingly slammed on a bar top. The shot glass can also stand in for a measure when making cocktails.

MARGARITA GLASS

The margarita, or coupette, glass, as its name implies, was designed specifically for serving margaritas. It's ideal for any frozen, blended drinks.

COUPE GLASS

A wide-rim glass that's good for serving sparkling drinks was once the glass of choice for champagne. Legend has it that the glass was inspired by the shape of a woman's breast.

HURRICANE GLASS

This pear-shaped glass pays homage to the hurricane lamp and was used to create the New Orleans rum-based cocktail: the Hurricane. It's also used for a variety of frozen and blended cocktails.

ICED BEVERAGE GLASS

A variation on the highball glass that combines a tapered, tall bowl with a short stem, this glass is ideal for serving chilled drinks.

EQUIPMENT

THE EQUIPMENT YOU HAVE in your home bar depends on whether you are a cocktail king or queen who likes all the latest gadgets, or whether you are prepared to make do with some basic options. Nowadays, there is no limit to the amount of bar equipment available, but you definitely won't need a lot of gimmicky gadgets to make the majority of the drinks in this book. Here is an outline of the essential tools of the trade.

JIGGERS

A jigger is a bartender's basic measuring tool and is essential for crafting the perfect blend of ingredients. It usually has a measurement on each end, such as 1 ounce and 1½ ounces. Look for a steel jigger with clear measurement markings so you can easily and accurately pour out the measures.

BARSPOON

A proper barspoon has a small bowl and a long handle that allows you to muddle, mix, and stir with ease. Spoons come in a variety of lengths and widths, and a stylish barspoon is an attractive addition to any bartender's equipment.

SHAKER

Most contemporary shakers are made from steel, because steel doesn't tarnish readily and doesn't conduct heat easily—this is useful for chilled cocktails, because the ice cools the cocktail instead of the shaker. Most standard shakers come with a built-in strainer, but if you're using a Boston or Parisian shaker, you'll need to use a separate strainer.

MIXING GLASS

Any vessel that holds about 2 cups of liquid can be used for mixing drinks. It's good to have a mixing glass with a spout or ridged rim so that you can stop ice from slipping into the glass; however, this is not vital, because you can always use a strainer. Mixing glasses are increasingly popular, and they are usually made of glass or crystal.

MUDDLER

For mashing up citrus fruit or crushing herbs, you need a muddler. This is a chunky wooden tool with a rounded end, and it can also be used to make cracked ice. You can mash fruit or crush herbs with a mortar and pestle, but the advantage of a muddler is that it can be used directly in the mixing glass.

STRAINER

A bar or Hawthorne strainer is an essential tool to prevent ice and other ingredients from being poured into your glass. Some cocktails need to be double strained, so even if there is a strainer in your cocktail shaker, you'll still need a separate Hawthorne strainer in your bar collection.

JUICER

A traditional juicer, with a ridged half-lemon shape on a saucer, works well for juicing small amounts. There is also a citrus spout available that screws into a lemon or lime; it's useful for obtaining tiny amounts of juice. Mechanical or electric presses are great for large amounts of juice, but they are not essential in a home bar.

OTHER EQUIPMENT

Other items you might need in your home bar equipment are a corkscrew, bottle opener, decorative toothpicks, blender, tongs, ice bucket, cutting board, knives, pitchers, swizzle sticks, straws, and an espuma gun for making foams.

MIXOLOGY TECHNIQUES

SHAKING AND STIRRING

These are the 2 most basic mixology techniques, and they are essential to master to confidently make a range of classic and craft cocktails.

Shaking is when you add all the ingredients, with the specified amount of ice cubes, to the shaker and shake vigorously for 5–10 seconds. The benefits of shaking are that the drink is rapidly mixed, chilled, and aerated. Once the drink has been shaken, the outside of the shaker should be lightly frosted.

Shaking a cocktail will dilute your drink significantly. This is an essential part of the cocktail-making process and gives recipes the correct balance of taste, strength, and temperature. After shaking, the drink is double strained into glasses—the shaker should have a built-in strainer, but you may also use a separate strainer over the glass. Shaking can also be used to prepare cocktails that include an ingredient that will not combine with less vigorous forms of mixing, such as an egg white.

Stirring is the purist's choice. This is a mixing technique where you add all the ingredients, usually with some ice cubes, but you combine them in a mixing glass and then stir the ingredients together using a long-handled barspoon or swizzle stick. This allows for you to blend and chill the ingredients without too much erosion of the ice, so you can control the level of dilution and keep it to a minimum.

BUILDING AND LAYERING

Building is a technique of pouring all the ingredients, one by one, usually over ice into the serving glass. You might then stir the cocktail briefly, but this is just to mix instead of to chill or aerate. The order the ingredients are added can change from drink to drink, which can affect the final flavor.

Another important bartending skill is the art of layering, requiring concentration, precision, and a steady hand. To make layered drinks, you generally pour the heaviest liquid first, working to the lightest. The real trick is the technique. Touch the top of the drink with a long-handled barspoon and pour the liquid slowly over the back of it to disperse it across the top of the ingredients already in the glass. Be sure to use a clean barspoon for each layer. Floating is the term used to describe adding the top layer.

MUDDLING AND BLENDING

Muddling is the extraction of the juice or oils from the pulp or skin of a fruit, herb, or spice and involves mashing ingredients to release their flavors. It's usually done with a wooden pestle-like implement called a muddler. (If you don't have a muddler, use a mortar and pestle or the end of a wooden spoon.) The best muddling technique is to keep pressing down with a twisting action until the ingredient has released all of its oil or juice.

Blending is when all the cocktail ingredients are combined in a blender or food processor. This technique is often used when mixing alcohol with fruit or with creamy ingredients that do not combine well otherwise. Use crushed or cracked ice to produce cocktails with a smooth, frozen consistency.

FOAMS

Foams and airs can be created in various thicknesses, from a light froth to a heavy, creamy foam. For a simple foam, use egg white, lemon juice, and sugar. To top 2 cocktails, whisk 1 egg white with ½ ounce of lemon juice and 1 teaspoon of granulated sugar until thoroughly mixed. Put the mixture into an espuma gun or cream whipper, then charge, shake, and spray it over the top of the cocktails for a light, creamy finish. The fresher the egg white, the more stable the foam, so use fresh eggs.

Chapter One

CLASSIC SPRITZ

You can never go wrong with a classic. From the famous Aperol spritz to the refreshing Hugo spritz, in this section you'll find original spritz cocktails made with traditional aperitifs.

APEROL SPRITZ

Serves 1

3 ounces prosecco
2 ounces Aperol
1 ounce club soda
orange slice, to garnish

1. In a large wine glass filled halfway with ice, add the prosecco followed by the Aperol liqueur

2. Top with the club soda. Garnish with an orange slice.

HUGO SPRITZ

Serves 1

½ ounce St-Germain elderflower liqueur
2 fresh mint sprigs, extra to garnish
4 ounces prosecco
1 ounce club soda
lemon slice, to garnish

1. Gently muddle the elderflower liqueur and 2 sprigs of mint in a wine glass.
2. Add ice to the glass, then top with prosecco and club soda. Stir gently to combine.
3. Garnish with a mint sprig and a lemon slice.

LILLET SPRITZ

Serves 1

2½ ounces Lillet Blanc
2½ ounces champagne or prosecco
orange slice, to garnish

1. Add the Lillet Blanc to a wine glass filled with ice.

2. Top with champagne or prosecco, then garnish with an orange slice.

PASTIS SPRITZ

Serves 1

1 ounce pastis
2 ounces prosecco
soda water, for topping
lemon wedge, to garnish

1. Pour the pastis and prosecco into a cocktail glass filled with ice.

2. Top with soda water, and garnish with a lemon wedge.

LEMONY OUZO MINT SPRITZER

Serves 1

3 sprigs fresh mint, extra to garnish
1 ounce lemon juice
½ ounce simple syrup
1 ounce ouzo
4 ounces prosecco
lemon slice, to garnish

1. Add the mint and lemon juice to a cocktail shaker, then muddle together.

2. Add ice, simple syrup, and ouzo, and shake until well mixed.

3. Strain into a cocktail glass filled with ice, top with prosecco, and garnish with fresh mint and a lemon slice.

THE GRAND 75

Serves 1

1½ ounces Grand Marnier
½ ounce lemon juice
3 ounces champagne
lemon peel, to garnish

1. Add the Grand Marnier and lemon juice to a champagne flute or coupe. Stir gently.

2. Top with champagne and stir gently again. Garnish with a twist of lemon peel.

COINTREAU SPRITZ

Serves 1

1 ounce Cointreau
2 ounces prosecco
1 ounce grapefruit soda
mint sprig, to garnish
orange slice, to garnish

1. Add the Cointreau, prosecco, and grapefruit soda to a cocktail glass filled halfway with ice. Stir gently.

2. Garnish with a mint sprig and orange slice.

AMARO SPRITZ

Serves 1

2 ounces amaro
3 ounces dry sparkling wine
1 ounce soda water
lime wedge, to garnish

1. Add the amaro to a cocktail glass filled with ice.

2. Top with sparkling wine and club soda. Stir gently.

3. Garnish with a lime wedge.

CITRUS SPRITZ

Serves 1

1½ ounces blanc vermouth
4 dashes orange bitters
½ ounce lemon juice
dry sparkling wine, for topping
rosemary sprig, to garnish
lemon slices, to garnish

1. Add the vermouth, bitters, and lemon juice to a cocktail glass filled with ice.

2. Top with sparkling wine to taste, then garnish with a rosemary sprig and lemon slices.

FROZEN APEROL SPRITZ

Serves 2

4 ounces orange juice
4 ounces Aperol
4 ounces prosecco
orange slices, to garnish

1. Add about 2 cups of ice to a blender, then add the orange juice and Aperol. Blend until fully combined.

2. Divide the mixture into 2 cocktail glasses, then top with prosecco.

3. Garnish each with an orange slice.

Chapter Two

LA VITA FRIZZANTE

It's time to indulge in *la vita frizzante*: the fizzy life. In this chapter you'll see twists on classic spritzes inspired by Italian flavors, like lemon, basil, and blood orange, and topped with something sparkling and bubbly.

LIMONCELLO SPRITZ

Serves 1

2 ounces limoncello
3 ounces prosecco
1 ounce club soda
lemon slices, to garnish

1. Fill a large wine glass halfway with ice. Add the limoncello, then top with prosecco and club soda.

2. Garnish with lemon slices.

CAMPARI SPRITZ

Serves 1

2 ounces Campari
3 ounces prosecco
1 ounce soda water
orange slice, to garnish

1. Add the Campari, prosecco, and soda to a wine glass filled with ice.

2. Garnish with an orange slice.

NEGRONI SPRITZ

Serves 2

8 ounces orange or blood orange juice
4 ounces Campari
4 ounces gin
4 ounces sweet vermouth
club soda, for topping
orange slice, to garnish

1. In a cocktail mixing glass, add the orange juice, Campari, gin, and vermouth, then mix well.

2. Stir in the club soda, then divide the mixture between 2 cocktail glasses.

3. Garnish with a slice of orange.

BLOOD ORANGE SPRITZ

Serves 1

2 ounces blood orange juice
3 ounces Aperol
4 ounces prosecco
1 ounce club soda or blood orange Italian soda
blood orange wedges, to garnish
sprig of fresh thyme, to garnish

1. Add the blood orange juice to a cocktail glass filled with ice.

2. Pour in the Aperol and prosecco. Stir gently.

3. Top with club soda or blood orange soda. Garnish with orange wedges and fresh sprig of thyme.

ITALIAN RED WINE SPRITZER

Serves 1

2 ounces sweet red wine
1 ounce Campari
2 ounces limonata (or Italian lemon soda)
1 orange wedge, to garnish

1. Add the red wine and Campari to a cocktail glass filled with ice. Stir gently.
2. Top with limonata, then garnish with an orange wedge.

THE VENETIAN SPRITZ

Serves 1

2 ounces Select Aperitivo
3 ounces prosecco
soda water, for topping
green olive, to garnish

1. Fill a large wine glass halfway with ice. Add the Select and prosecco, then stir gently.

2. Top with soda water and garnish with a green olive on a toothpick.

CAPPELLETTI SPRITZ

Serves 1

2 ounces Cappelletti
¾ ounce rose lemonade
4 ounces prosecco
soda water, for topping
lemon slice, to garnish
mint sprigs, to garnish

1. Add the Cappelletti and rose lemonade to a cocktail glass filled with ice. Stir gently.

2. Add the prosecco, then top with soda water. Garnish with a lemon slice and fresh mint.

BASIL SPRITZ

Serves 1

1½ ounces elderflower liqueur
fresh basil, plus extra to garnish
1 ounce simple syrup
1 ounce lemon juice
3 ounces sparkling wine
soda water, for topping

1. Add the elderflower liqueur and a few basil leaves to a cocktail shaker. Muddle until flavors combine.

2. Add ice, simple syrup, and lemon juice, and shake until well combined.

3. Strain into a cocktail glass, top with sparkling wine and a splash of soda water, and garnish with a basil leaf.

LEMON FIZZ

Serves 1

4 ounces limonata (or Italian lemon soda)
1½ ounces gin
sparkling wine, for topping
mint sprig, to garnish
lemon slice, to garnish

1. Add the limonata and gin to a cocktail glass filled with ice. Stir to mix.

2. Top with sparkling wine to taste, then garnish with a mint sprig and lemon slice.

Chapter Three

FRESHLY SQUEEZED

This chapter provides a refreshing collection of drinks made with fruit juice and bright flavors. From peach and passion fruit juices to classic orange, these drinks provide a fresh twist for the palate.

RUBY RED SPRITZ

Serves 1

1 ounce dry gin
1 ounce Ruby Red grapefruit juice
½ ounce Campari
3 ounces dry sparkling rosé, chilled
club soda, for topping
sprig of thyme, to garnish
grapefruit wedge, to garnish

1. Add the gin, grapefruit juice, and Campari to a cocktail glass filled with ice.

2. Top with sparkling rosé and club soda, then stir gently. Garnish with fresh thyme and a grapefruit wedge.

PEACH PALOMA SPRITZ

Serves 1

2 ounces tequila
1 ounce lime juice
2 ounces peach nectar
soda water, for topping
peach slices (fresh or canned), to garnish
rosemary sprig, to garnish

1. Add the tequila, lime juice, and peach nectar to a cocktail shaker filled with ice. Shake until the mixture is chilled.

2. Strain into a cocktail glass filled with ice, then top with soda water. Garnish with peach slices and a sprig of rosemary.

LYCHEE SPRITZ

Serves 1

1½ ounces lychee liqueur
3 ounces prosecco
½ teaspoon lime juice
fresh lychee, to garnish, optional
fresh mint, to garnish

1. Add the lychee liqueur to a cocktail glass filled with ice. Add the prosecco and lime juice, then stir gently.

2. Float fresh lychee in the drink, if you'd like, and garnish with mint leaves.

CRANBERRY SPRITZ

Serves 1

3 ounces champagne or prosecco
1 ounce Aperol
1 ounce cranberry juice
fresh cranberries, to garnish
lemon slice, to garnish
sprig of rosemary, to garnish

1. Add the champagne or prosecco, Aperol, and cranberry juice to a wine glass filled with ice. Gently stir.

2. Garnish with fresh cranberries, a lemon slice, and fresh rosemary.

SPARKLING STRAWBERRY

Serves 1

3 strawberries, plus ½ to garnish
2 ounces pineapple juice
2 teaspoons lime juice
3½ ounces ginger beer
2 ounces prosecco or sparkling wine
lime wedge, to garnish

1. Muddle the strawberries in a copper mug or a highball glass.
2. Add the pineapple juice and lime juice. Stir well to mix.
3. Add ice, then top with ginger beer and prosecco or sparkling wine. Garnish with a strawberry half and a lime wedge.

PEAR ROSEMARY SPRITZER

Serves 1

1½ ounces pear juice
1 teaspoon rosemary simple syrup
1 ounce lemon-lime soda
champagne or prosecco, for topping
pear slice, to garnish
sprig of rosemary, to garnish

ROSEMARY SIMPLE SYRUP
4 ounces water
½ cup granulated sugar
4 sprigs of rosemary

1. To make the rosemary simple syrup, add water, sugar, and fresh rosemary to a small saucepan over medium heat. Bring to a boil and stir until sugar is completely dissolved. Remove from heat and allow to completely cool. Strain syrup into an airtight container and store in the refrigerator for up to 2 weeks.

2. Add the pear juice, simple syrup, and lemon-lime soda to a cocktail glass filled with ice.

3. Fill the rest of the glass with champagne or prosecco. Gently stir, then garnish with a pear slice and fresh rosemary.

THE GREEN GODDESS

Serves 1

½ kiwi, peeled
2 ounces gin
¾ ounce elderflower liqueur
½ ounce lime juice
1 ounce simple syrup
soda water, for topping
kiwi slice, to garnish

1. In a cocktail shaker, add the kiwi and gin, then muddle until the kiwi has broken down.

2. Add the elderflower liqueur, lime juice, and simple syrup, and shake until well combined.

3. Strain the mixture into a cocktail glass filled with ice. Top with soda water, then garnish with a kiwi slice.

PASSION FRUIT FIZZ

Serves 1

1½ ounces gin
2 ounces passion fruit juice
2 tablespoons passion fruit pulp
5–6 drops of lemon bitters
soda water, for topping
lemon slice, to garnish
sprig of rosemary, to garnish

1. Add the gin, passion fruit juice and pulp, and lemon bitters to a cocktail glass filled with ice.

2. Top with soda water and gently stir. Garnish with a lemon slice and fresh rosemary.

CRANBERRY-ORANGE APEROL

Serves 1

2 ounces cranberry juice
2 ounces Aperol
3 ounces champagne or prosecco
1 ounce club soda
orange slice, to garnish
fresh cranberries, to garnish

1. Add the cranberry juice, Aperol, and champagne or prosecco to a cocktail glass filled with ice.

2. Top with club soda, then garnish with an orange slice and fresh cranberries.

SUNSET SPRITZ

Serves 2

1 watermelon, chopped and seeded, extra cubed pieces to garnish, optional
3 ounces grapefruit juice
3 ounces orange juice
½ ounce lime juice
4 ounces gin
champagne or prosecco, for topping
lemon or lime slices, to garnish
mint sprigs, to garnish

1. Add the melon to a blender with the grapefruit juice, orange juice, lime juice, and gin. Blend until smooth.

2. Pour into cocktail glasses and top with champagne or prosecco. Float small pieces of watermelon in the drink, if you'd like, and garnish with slices of lemon or lime and mint leaves.

Chapter Four

POP THE CHAMPAGNE

Whether you're celebrating an engagement, a new job, or just a Tuesday after work, these champagne cocktails are perfect for brightening all of life's moments, big and small.

FRENCH 75

Serves 1

1 ounce gin
½ ounce lemon juice
½ ounce simple syrup
3 ounces champagne
lemon twist, to garnish

1. In a cocktail shaker filled with ice, add the gin, lemon juice, and simple syrup. Shake until well chilled, then strain into a champagne flute or coupe.

2. Top with champagne. Garnish with a lemon twist.

BLUEBERRY-ORANGE SPRITZ

Serves 1

1½ ounces Cointreau
½ ounce lemon juice
8 blueberries, plus extra to garnish
2 ounces soda water
2 ounces champagne
mint leaves, to garnish

1. In a cocktail shaker filled with ice, add the Cointreau, lemon juice, and blueberries. Muddle until the blueberries have broken down.

2. Strain into a cocktail glass filled with ice, then top with soda water and sparkling wine. Gently stir.

3. Float blueberries in the drink and garnish with fresh mint.

MELON BELLINI

Serves 1

2 ounces pureed watermelon
½ teaspoon agave syrup
2 teaspoons apple juice
2 ounces ginger ale
3 ounces champagne
thin watermelon slice, to garnish

1. In a cocktail shaker filled with ice, add the watermelon puree, agave syrup, and apple juice. Shake until well combined.

2. Strain into a chilled champagne flute and top with ginger ale and champagne.

3. Garnish with a watermelon slice.

GIN, CHAMPAGNE & GRAPEFRUIT SORBET COCKTAIL

Serves 6

3 cups grapefruit sorbet (or any preferred flavor sorbet)
6 ounces gin
12 dashes rhubarb bitters
1 (750 mL) bottle champagne
6 grapefruit peel twists, to garnish

1. Add ½ cup of sorbet to each of the 6 cocktail glasses. Then add 1 ounce of gin and 2 dashes of rhubarb bitters to each glass.

2. Top with the champagne and garnish with the grapefruit peel twists.

ELDERFLOWER CHAMPAGNE FIZZ

Serves 1

1 ounce elderflower liqueur
½ ounce vodka
5 ounces chilled champagne

1. Pour the elderflower liqueur into a champagne flute.
2. Add the vodka, then top with champagne.

BELLINI

Serves 1

¾ ounce peach juice
3 ounces champagne, chilled

1. Pour the peach juice into a champagne flute.

2. Top with champagne.

CAMPARI GIN FIZZ

Serves 1

1½ ounces gin
¾ ounce Campari
¾ ounce fresh lemon juice
½ ounce simple syrup
1 large egg white
1 ounce champagne
 or prosecco
lemon slice, to garnish

1. In a cocktail shaker filled with ice, add the gin, Campari, lemon juice, simple syrup, and egg white. Shake well until frothy.

2. Strain into a cocktail glass. Top with champagne or prosecco, and garnish with lemon slice.

THE FIZZY PEAR

Serves 1

2 ounces Calvados
2 ounces pear nectar or
1 ounce pear liqueur
champagne, chilled,
for topping
pear slice, to garnish

1. Pour the Calvados and pear nectar into a chilled glass filled with ice.
2. Top with chilled champagne and garnish with a pear slice.

CHAMPAGNE SPARKLER

Serves 1

3 drops Angostura bitters
6 ounces champagne
lime slice, to garnish

1. Add the bitters to a champagne flute.
2. Pour the champagne and garnish with a slice of lime.

KIR ROYALE

Serves 1

½ ounce creme de cassis
champagne, for topping
fresh raspberries, to garnish

1. Pour the creme de cassis into a champagne flute.

2. Top with champagne, then garnish with a few fresh raspberries.

Chapter Five

BUBBLY BRUNCH

Few matches are better than brunch paired with a glass of something bubbly. Here you'll find spritzy cocktails, perfect for serving in the morning, from a classic Mimosa to a Cold Brew Spritzer.

MIMOSA

Serves 1

4 ounces champagne, prosecco, or sparkling wine
2 ounces orange juice
orange slice, to garnish

1. Pour champagne into a chilled flute, then add the orange juice.

2. Garnish with an orange slice.

TOMATO SPRITZ

Serves 1

8 cherry or grape tomatoes, 2 reserved for garnish, chopped in half
1–2 basil leaves, 2 extra to garnish
2 ounces Lillet blanc
1 ounce grapefruit juice
1 ounce gin
3 ounces prosecco or sparkling wine

1. Muddle the tomatoes and basil in a cocktail shaker. Add ice, Lillet, grapefruit juice, and gin. Shake until well combined.

2. Strain into a cocktail glass filled with ice, then top with prosecco or sparkling wine.

3. Garnish with chopped tomatoes and basil leaves.

CAPRESE SPRITZ

Serves 1

5 cherry tomatoes,
2 reserved for garnish
2 basil leaves, plus
extra for garnish
1 ounce Campari
1 teaspoon balsamic vinegar
pinch of salt
2 ounces lemon soda
3 ounces prosecco or
sparkling wine
bocconcini, to garnish

1. Add tomatoes, basil leaves, Campari, balsamic vinegar, and salt to a cocktail shaker, then muddle until tomatoes have released their juices.

2. Add ice and shake until well combined.

3. Strain into a wine glass and top with lemon soda and prosecco.

4. Garnish with a caprese skewer made from reserved tomatoes, basil leaves, and bocconcini.

MAPLE BOURBON APEROL SPRITZ

Serves 1

1½ ounces bourbon
1 ounce Aperol
1 ounce pure maple syrup
3 ounces prosecco
orange slice, to garnish

1. Combine bourbon, Aperol, and maple syrup in a cocktail shaker filled with ice. Shake until maple syrup has dissolved.

2. Pour into a lowball glass filled with ice.

3. Top with prosecco and garnish with an orange slice.

COLD BREW SPRITZER

Serves 1

4 ounces tonic or sparkling water
4 ounces cold brew concentrate
2 ounces amaretto
squeeze of lemon juice
lemon slice to garnish

1. Add tonic or sparkling water to a tall glass filled halfway with ice.

2. In a cocktail mixing glass, add the cold brew concentrate, amaretto, and lemon juice. Mix to combine.

3. Float the amaretto cold brew to the tall glass of tonic or sparkling water. Garnish with a lemon slice.

PEACHY THYME SPRITZ

Serves 1

½ cup canned peaches in light syrup
1 teaspoon fresh thyme
1 ounce elderflower liqueur
1 ounce peach nectar
prosecco or champagne, for topping
peach slices, to garnish
fresh thyme sprigs, to garnish

1. Add the peaches with syrup and fresh thyme to a cocktail shaker. Muddle until peaches have broken down and thyme has mixed into the syrup.

2. Add ice to the cocktail shaker along with the elderflower liqueur and peach nectar. Shake until well mixed.

3. Strain into a cocktail glass filled halfway with ice and top with prosecco or champagne. Garnish with peach slices and fresh thyme.

BROWN SUGAR ESPRESSO TONIC

Serves 1

1½ ounces brewed espresso, cooled
1 ounce bourbon
1 ounce coffee liqueur
2 tablespoons brown sugar simple syrup
club soda, for topping

BROWN SUGAR SIMPLE SYRUP
1 cup brown sugar
1 cup water

1. To make the syrup, add the brown sugar and water to a saucepan over medium heat. Cook, stirring occasionally, until the sugar has dissolved. Don't let the mixture come to a boil, otherwise the syrup will crystallize. Remove from heat and allow syrup to fully cool. Transfer to an air-tight container. The syrup can be stored in the refrigerator for 3–4 weeks.

2. In a cocktail shaker filled with ice, add the cooled espresso, bourbon, coffee liqueur, brown sugar syrup, and shake to combine.

3. Pour into a cocktail glass, and top with club soda.

Chapter Six

EFFERVESCENT MOCKTAILS

In this section you'll find mocktails that embrace fresh produce and ingredients that are light and refreshing, but still pack a fizzy punch.

CUCUMBER ROSE MOCKTAIL

Serves 2

1 English cucumber, juiced
1½ ounces lemon juice
1 ounce rose simple syrup
club soda, for topping
cucumber slice, to garnish
mint sprig, to garnish

ROSE SIMPLE SYRUP
4 ounces water
2 cups granulated sugar
4 ounces rose water

1. To make the syrup, bring water to a boil in a saucepan over medium-high heat. Add the sugar and stir until dissolved. Stir in the rose water, lower the heat to medium-low, and cover. Simmer for 15 minutes.

2. When the syrup has thickened, pour into an airtight container. The syrup will stay fresh for up to 2–3 weeks in the refrigerator.

3. In a cocktail shaker filled with ice, add the cucumber juice, lemon juice, and rose simple syrup. Shake well to combine.

4. Pour into 2 Collins glasses filled with ice, and top with club soda. Garnish with a cucumber slice and fresh mint.

LAVENDER SPARKLER

Serves 1

1 ounce lavender syrup
4 ounces fresh lemonade
3 ounces club soda
lavender sprig, to garnish

1. In a highball glass filled halfway with ice, add the lavender syrup and lemonade. Stir to mix.

2. Top with club soda. Garnish with a lavender sprig.

POMEGRANATE & ROSE REFRESHER

Serves 8–10

8–10 fresh mint sprigs, to garnish (optional)
sparkling water, to serve

POMEGRANATE AND ROSE SYRUP
juice of 2 lemons
¼ teaspoon rose water
7 ounces fresh pomegranate juice (juice of about 2 pomegranates)
¾ cup sugar

1. To make the syrup, put the lemon juice, rose water, pomegranate juice, and sugar in a saucepan. Stir and cook over low heat until the sugar has dissolved.

2. Increase the heat to medium-high, bring to a boil, then reduce the heat to low and simmer for 3–4 minutes. Boiling sugar is very hot, so handle with care and make sure it doesn't bubble over. Leave to cool completely. The syrup will keep in the refrigerator in a sealed container for 3–4 days.

3. Put some crushed ice in a tall glass. Pour 1 dash of the syrup over the ice and add a sprig of mint, if using. Pour in still or sparkling water to taste, and mix well.

FRESH MINT SPARKLER

Serves 1

6 fresh mint leaves, plus extra to garnish
1 teaspoon sugar
3 ounces lemon juice
sparkling water
lemon slice, to garnish

1. Put the mint leaves into a chilled Collins or highball glass.
2. Add the sugar and lemon juice.
3. Muddle the mint leaves and stir until the sugar has dissolved.
4. Fill the glass with ice cubes and top with sparkling water. Stir gently and garnish with the fresh mint and lemon slice.

PINK POMEGRANATE

Serves 1

5 teaspoons pomegranate juice, chilled
4 ounces ginger ale, chilled
1 teaspoon pomegranate seeds, to garnish

1. Pour the pomegranate juice into a champagne flute.
2. Top with chilled ginger ale. Garnish with the pomegranate seeds.

VIRGIN COOLER

Serves 1

2 teaspoons sugar
lime wedge
2 ounces grenadine
2 ounces fresh lemon or lime juice
lemonade
fresh lemon or lime slices, to garnish

1. Pour the sugar on a saucer. Rub the rim of a chilled highball glass with the lime wedge, then twist the glass rim into the sugar to frost. Fill halfway with ice.

2. Pour the grenadine and citrus juice into the ice-filled glass.

3. Top with lemonade and garnish with slices of lemon or lime.

CHERRY TWIST

Serves 1

juice of 1 lemon or ½ pink grapefruit
1 ounce grenadine
zest of ½ lemon
2–3 teaspoons cherry syrup
soda water, for topping
maraschino cherry, to garnish

1. Pour the lemon or grapefruit juice and grenadine into a Collins glass with ice.

2. Add the lemon zest, syrup, and soda water to taste. Garnish with a cherry.

JUNIPER JULEP

Serves 4

8½ cups white grape juice
¼ ounce (about 40) food-grade juniper berries
2 teaspoons agave syrup
8 teaspoons fresh lime juice
20 fresh mint leaves
4 fresh mint sprigs, to garnish
8 juniper berries, to garnish

1. Pour the grape juice into a pitcher. Add the juniper berries, stir well, then leave to infuse for 3 hours. Strain the juice into a clean bottle and store in the refrigerator for up to 1 month.

2. Mix the agave syrup and lime juice in a cocktail shaker to dissolve the syrup.

3. Bruise the mint leaves and add to the cocktail shaker.

4. Fill the shaker with crushed ice, then pour in 16 ounces of the infused grape juice. Shake to combine.

5. Divide the mixture between 4 julep cups or highball glasses, then top with more crushed ice. Garnish each glass with a mint sprig and 2 juniper berries.

BITTER FIZZ

Serves 1

2 ounces lime juice
2 teaspoons nonalcoholic aromatic bitters, or to taste
3½ ounces nonalcoholic ginger beer
3½ ounces lemonade
lime slice, to garnish

1. Mix all the ingredients together in a highball glass.

2. Taste and add more bitters if you wish.

3. Garnish with a lime slice.

PINEAPPLE PIZZAZZ

Serves 1

juice of ½ orange
juice of 1 lime
5 ounces pineapple juice
4–5 drops nonalcoholic aromatic bitters, extra to taste
sparkling water or ginger ale, to taste
fruit slices, to garnish

1. In a cocktail shaker filled with ice, combine the first 4 ingredients and shake well.
2. Strain into a chilled glass and fill with sparkling water or ginger ale to taste.
3. Finish with a few more drops of bitters to taste, garnish with slices of fruit.

Chapter Seven

TIME TO PARTY

The guests are about to arrive—it's time to party! This chapter provides a fun collection of large-batch punches and spritzy cocktails ready for sharing with a big group.

PINEAPPLE & MINT ICED TEA

Serves 8

2 pineapples, reserve some for garnish
7 cups water
2 ounces fresh mint
4-inch piece of fresh ginger, peeled and finely sliced
8 ounces agave syrup
4 tablespoons fresh mint leaves, to garnish
750 mL bottle of champagne or prosecco, for topping

1. Prepare the pineapple by slicing off the base and leaves with a sharp knife. Rest the pineapple on its base and slice off the peel, until you reveal the flesh. Slice the fruit in half and remove the woody core that sits down the center. Cut the remaining flesh into ¾-inch cubes.

2. Pour the water into a large saucepan and add the pineapple, mint, and ginger. Stir in the agave syrup and place the saucepan over a medium-high heat. Simmer for 45 minutes, or until the liquid has reduced by half.

3. Remove from the heat and allow the nectar to cool completely and infuse. This will take 4–5 hours. Using a slotted spoon, remove the mint sprigs and ginger.

4. Add ice, mint leaves, and reserved pineapple cubes to the bottom of cocktail glasses, then pour in the cooled nectar, divided evenly between all glasses. Top with champagne or prosecco.

GRAPEFRUIT COOLERS

Serves 6

2 ounces fresh mint
3 ounces simple syrup
16 ounces grapefruit juice
6 ounces lemon juice
champagne or prosecco, for topping
fresh mint sprigs, to garnish

1. Muddle fresh mint leaves in a small bowl with the simple syrup.
2. Set aside for at least 2 hours to steep, mashing again from time to time.
3. Strain the steeped mixture into a pitcher and add the grapefruit juice and lemon juice. Cover with plastic wrap and chill for at least 2 hours.
4. To serve, fill 6 chilled Collins glasses with ice. Divide the grapefruit mixture evenly in the glasses, then top with champagne or prosecco. Garnish with fresh mint.

HEAVENLY DAYS

Serves 8

24 ounces hazelnut syrup
24 ounces lemon juice
8 teaspoons grenadine
champagne or prosecco, for topping
slices of papaya, to garnish

1. In a large pitcher filled with ice, add the syrup, lemon juice, and grenadine, and mix until well combined.

2. Fill 8 glasses halfway with ice, then strain the cocktail into the glasses.

3. Top with champagne or prosecco. Stir gently and garnish with a slice of papaya.

RASPBERRY COOLERS

Serves 8

2 tablespoons raspberry syrup
48 ounces apple juice, chilled
sparkling wine, for topping
fresh raspberries, to garnish
apple slices, to garnish

1. In a cocktail mixing glass filled with ice, add the raspberry syrup and apple juice. Stir to mix.

2. Fill each cocktail glass halfway with ice, then add 6 ounces of the raspberry and apple juice mixture.

3. Top each glass with sparkling wine. Garnish with the raspberries and slices of apple.

SPIKED RASPBERRY LEMONADE

Serves 8

4 lemons
2 cups confectioners' sugar
2 cups raspberries
1 teaspoon vanilla extract
champagne or prosecco, for topping
fresh mint sprigs, to garnish

1. Cut the ends off the lemons, then scoop out and chop the flesh.

2. Add the lemon flesh to a blender with the sugar, raspberries, vanilla extract, and ice. Blend for 2–3 minutes.

3. Fill 8 highball glasses halfway with ice, then strain in the blended mixture.

4. Top with champagne or prosecco, and garnish with mint sprigs.

CHAMPAGNE PUNCH

Serves 20

48 ounces pomegranate juice
16 ounces orange juice
¾ cup triple sec
12 ounces ginger ale
2 (750 mL) bottles champagne
2 oranges, thinly sliced into rounds, to garnish
pomegranate seeds, to garnish
rosemary sprigs, to garnish

1. Fill a large punch bowl with ice, then add the chilled pomegranate juice, orange juice, triple sec, ginger ale, and champagne. Stir gently to combine.

2. Garnish with orange slices, pomegranate seeds, and rosemary sprigs.

SUMMER SPRITZ PUNCH

Serves 12

24 ounces apple juice
12 ounces lemon juice
4 ounces simple syrup
32 ounces ginger ale
32 ounces prosecco or sparkling wine
orange slices, to garnish

1. Pour the apple juice into a large pitcher filled with ice, then add the lemon juice and simple syrup.

2. Add the ginger ale and prosecco or sparkling wine, and stir gently to mix.

3. Pour into chilled lowball glasses and garnish with orange slices.

APEROL SPRITZ PITCHER

Serves 6

24 ounces prosecco
16 ounces Aperol
8 ounces soda water
orange slices, to garnish

1. Add the prosecco and Aperol to a pitcher filled halfway with ice and several orange slices.

2. Top the pitcher with soda water and gently stir.

3. Serve in large wine glasses and garnish each with an orange slice.

RASPBERRY LEMONADE SPRITZES

Serves 8

40 ounces raspberry lemonade
18 ounces elderflower liqueur
1 (750 mL) bottle prosecco, chilled
mint leaves, to garnish
raspberries, to garnish
lemon slices, to garnish

1. In a pitcher filled halfway with ice, add the raspberry lemonade and elderflower liqueur. Stir to combine.

2. Pour the mixture into cocktail glasses, then top each with prosecco. Garnish with fresh mint, raspberries, and lemon slices.

PROSECCO MARGARITAS

Serves 6

9 ounces tequila
9 ounces Cointreau
6 ounces simple syrup, or to taste
8 ounces lime juice
1 bottle (750 mL) prosecco, chilled
lime wedges, to garnish
salt, to garnish

1. Rub a wedge of lime around the rim of each cocktail glass. Add salt to a small dish, then dip each cocktail glass into the salt to coat the rim.

2. In a pitcher filled with ice, add the tequila, Cointreau, simple syrup, and lime juice. Stir to combine.

3. Divide the mixture into the cocktail glasses, top each with prosecco, and garnish with a lime wedge.

Chapter Eight

SPARKLING CLASSICS

This chapter is all about reimagining classic cocktails as their sparkling counterparts. With the addition of sparkling wine, a traditional Manhattan becomes a Bustling Manhattan, and when topped with prosecco or champagne, a Cosmopolitan becomes A Bright Cosmo.

MOJITO SPRITZ

Serves 1

1½ ounces light rum
½ ounce lime juice
10–12 mint leaves, reserve some to garnish
½ ounce simple syrup
3 ounces sparkling wine

1. Add the rum, lime juice, mint, and simple syrup to a cocktail shaker. Muddle the ingredients together to infuse the mint.

2. Strain into a cocktail glass filled with ice, top with sparkling wine, and garnish with fresh mint.

CHAMPAGNE GIN FIZZ

Serves 1

2 ounces gin
1 tablespoon fresh lemon juice
1 teaspoon simple syrup or confectioners' sugar
1 egg white
champagne, for topping
lemon slice, to garnish

1. In a cocktail shaker filled with ice, add the gin, lemon juice, simple syrup, and egg white. Shake until frothy.

2. Pour into a cocktail glass filled with ice, top with champagne, and garnish with a lemon slice.

SPARKLING FRENCH MARTINI

Serves 1

2 ounces vodka
1 ounce Chambord liqueur
2 ounces pineapple juice
prosecco, chilled,
for topping
lemon twist, to garnish

1. In a cocktail shaker filled with ice, add the vodka, Chambord, and pineapple juice. Shake until well chilled.

2. Strain into a martini glass, top with prosecco, and garnish with a lemon twist.

BUSTLING MANHATTAN

Serves 1

2 ounces rye whiskey
1 ounce sweet vermouth
2 dashes Angostura bitters
sparkling wine, for topping
brandied cherry, to garnish

1. In a cocktail mixing glass, stir together the rye whiskey, sweet vermouth, and bitters until well chilled.

2. Strain into a chilled coupe glass, then top with sparkling wine and garnish with a brandied cherry.

SPARKLING LEMON DROP

Serves 1

1½ ounces lemon vodka
2 ounces lemon juice
½ ounce simple syrup
2 ounces champagne
or prosecco
lemon twist, to garnish

1. In a cocktail shaker filled with ice, add the vodka, lemon juice, and simple syrup. Shake until well chilled.

2. Strain into a martini glass, top with champagne or prosecco, and garnish with a lemon twist.

SPARKLING GIMLET

Serves 1

3 ounces gin
juice from 1 lime
2 ounces elderflower liqueur
champagne, for topping
lime twist, to garnish

1. Add the gin, lime juice, and elderflower liqueur to a cocktail shaker filled with ice. Shake until well combined.

2. Strain into a cocktail glass, top with champagne, and garnish with a lime twist.

A BRIGHT COSMO

Serves 1

1½ ounces of vodka
½ ounce of triple sec
½ ounce of lime juice
½ ounce of cranberry juice
1 ounce of prosecco or champagne, for topping
lime twist, to garnish

1. In a cocktail shaker filled with ice, add vodka, triple sec, lime juice, and cranberry juice. Shake until combined.

2. Strain into a martini glass, and top with prosecco or champagne. Garnish with a lime twist.

Chapter Nine

ON THE PATIO

Among this collection of spritz cocktails, you'll find some delicious recipes that pair well with the cocktails included in this book. From appetizers to salty snacks, there's bound to be something for everyone to enjoy on the patio with their aperitif of choice.

ANTIPASTO BOARD

Serves 6

DAIRY
brie
feta, cubed

MEAT
salami
soppressata

GRAINS
sesame seed crackers
sea salt snack crackers

FRUITS & VEGETABLES
green olives
red grapes

DIPPING SAUCES OR SPREADS
honey
stone ground mustard

OTHER ADDITIONS
candied pecans
roasted almonds
roasted peanuts
chocolate pieces

GARNISHES
rosemary sprigs
pomegranate seeds

1. Start by placing your cheeses on the board. Typically, it's best to place them on opposite ends of the board, which allows for more visual interest and variance of flavors and textures once the board is complete.

2. Next fold and place your meats around the board. There are a variety of ways to fold and display these, depending on the type of meat, like folding each piece in half, fanning, or stacking. Meat can even be displayed in shapes, like a rosette.

3. Now you can fill in the extra spaces and gaps with stacks or rows of crackers, grapes, nuts, olives, chocolate, and little bowls of honey and mustard.

4. Garnish with fresh rosemary sprigs and pomegranate seeds.

HERBY OLIVES

Serves 10
Prep: 5 mins

3½ cups mixed olives, drained and pitted
½ cup olive oil
zest of 1 lemon
1 teaspoon chili flakes
2 sprigs of fresh rosemary, finely chopped
2 tablespoons fresh thyme, chopped
4 garlic cloves, minced

1. To make the marinade, add the olive oil, lemon zest, chili flakes, rosemary, thyme, and minced garlic to a small bowl. Mix to combine.

2. Pour the marinade over the olives in another bowl, and mix to coat. Store in an airtight container in the refrigerator for up to 2 weeks.

HOMEMADE POTATO CHIPS

Serves 8–10
Prep: 40 mins • Cook: 20 mins

1 quart oil for frying
4 medium potatoes
3 tablespoons salt, plus more to taste

1. Use a mandoline to slice potatoes into paper-thin pieces, adding them to a bowl of cold water as they're cut.

2. Drain slices and rinse under cold water. Refill the bowl with water, add the salt, and return the potatoes to the bowl. Soak for 30 minutes, then drain and rinse the potatoes, and pat dry.

3. Heat oil in a large pot over high heat until it reaches about 365°F.

4. Fry the potato slices in small batches (with enough chips to cover the top of the oil) until they're golden in color. Chips should not be completely brown, but golden-brown around the edges with the bubbling subsiding.

5. When they've reached the desired color, remove from the pot using a mesh straining spoon and drain on paper towels. Season with salt to taste.

WHIPPED RICOTTA WITH HOT HONEY

Serves 4
Prep: 5 mins

WHIPPED RICOTTA

2 cups fresh ricotta (about 475g)
zest from half a lemon
juice from half a lemon
¼ teaspoon salt
¼ teaspoon ground pepper
1 tablespoon olive oil

HOT HONEY

¼ cup honey
1 teaspoon hot sauce
½ teaspoon chili flakes

crackers or crostini, to serve

1. Add the ricotta, lemon zest, lemon juice, salt, pepper, and olive oil to a food processor. Blend until smooth, transfer to a serving bowl, then set aside.

2. In a small bowl, mix together the honey, hot sauce, and chili flakes.

3. Drizzle the honey mixture over the ricotta. Serve with crackers or crostini.

HONEY SPICED NUTS

Serves 6
Bake: 10 mins

½ cup Brazil nuts
½ cup pecans
½ cup cashew nuts
2 tablespoons pumpkin seeds
1 tablespoon sunflower oil
1½ tablespoons honey
½ teaspoon ground cinnamon
½ teaspoon allspice
½ teaspoon black pepper
½ teaspoon sweet paprika
¼ teaspoon salt

1. Line a baking sheet with parchment paper and preheat the oven to 275°F.

2. Reserving half of the honey for later, combine all ingredients in a bowl and mix. Then spread the mixture on the prepared baking sheet.

3. Place on the middle shelf of the oven and cook for 10 minutes. Remove from the oven, then drizzle the remaining honey over the nuts. Let cool before serving. Store in an airtight container for up to 1 week.

GARLIC BREAD TWISTS

Serves 15
Prep: 10 mins • Bake: 8–10 mins

1 (1-pound) package
premade pizza dough
½ cup butter, melted
⅛ cup Parmesan
cheese, grated
1 tablespoon dried parsley
1 tablespoon garlic, minced
1 teaspoon garlic salt
cornmeal, for sprinkling

1. Preheat the oven to 450°F.

2. Cut the dough into 15 dough balls of the same size. Roll each ball into a long rope, about 6 inches by 1 inch. You can add a little twist or leave it straight.

3. In a bowl, mix together the melted butter, cheese, parsley, garlic, and garlic salt. Brush the mixture over each piece of dough.

4. Sprinkle a baking sheet with some cornmeal, then place the bread sticks on the sheet.

5. Bake for 8–10 minutes or until golden brown. Remove from the oven and coat the twists again with the butter mixture.

EGGPLANT CAPONATA

Serves 6
Prep: 25 mins • Cook: 40 mins

- 2 tablespoons olive oil
- 1 medium onion, chopped
- 2 stalks celery, diced
- 3 garlic cloves, minced
- 2 red bell peppers, diced
- 1 teaspoon salt, plus more to taste
- 1 large eggplant, roasted until tender, and coarsely chopped
- 1 pound Roma tomatoes, peeled, seeded, and finely chopped
- 2 tablespoons sugar, extra pinch reserved
- 3 tablespoons capers, rinsed and drained
- 3 tablespoons green olives, pitted and coarsely chopped
- 3 tablespoons red or white wine vinegar
- pepper, to taste

1. Heat 1 tablespoon of the oil in a large skillet over medium heat, then add the onion and celery. Stir while cooking until the onion softens, then add the garlic. Cook until the garlic becomes fragrant, about 30 seconds.

2. Add the peppers and ½ teaspoon of salt to the skillet. Stir while cooking until the peppers are just about tender, then add another tablespoon of oil and the eggplant. Cook for another 5 minutes until the vegetables are tender and the eggplant is falling apart.

3. Add the tomatoes, another ½ teaspoon of salt, and a pinch of sugar. Cook, scraping the bottom of the pan often, until the tomatoes have cooked down.

4. Add the capers, olives, remaining sugar, and vinegar. Turn down the heat and cook for 20 to 30 minutes, stirring often, until the vegetables are completely cooked and the mixture has thickened considerably.
5. Remove from heat, and season to taste with salt and pepper. Serve at room temperature with crusty bread.

ROSEMARY FOCACCIA

Serves 4
Prep: 25 mins • Bake: 20 mins

3 cups unbleached all-purpose flour
1½ teaspoons salt
1 teaspoon granulated sugar
1 teaspoon instant yeast
1¼ cups warm water
1½ tablespoons extra-virgin olive oil, plus more for drizzling
2 sprigs fresh rosemary
sea salt, to top

1. In a large bowl whisk together the flour, salt, sugar, and yeast. Add the water and olive oil, then stir until combined. Cover the bowl and set aside for 15 minutes.

2. With a wet hand, grab a section of dough from one side of the bowl, then lift it up and press it into the center. Repeat this motion, grabbing a new section of dough each time, until you've made a full circle around the bowl. Flip the dough over so the smooth side is up. Cover again and let the dough rest for 15 minutes.

3. Repeat the bowl fold method 3 more times (4 times total), each time covering the bowl and letting the dough rest for another 15 minutes. After the fourth time, the dough should feel pretty strong. Cover the bowl and let the dough rise for 1 hour, after which the dough should have doubled in size.

4. Spray the bottom and sides of a 9-inch square baking dish with nonstick spray. Line with parchment paper and spray again with nonstick spray. Then add 1 tablespoon of olive oil, making sure it covers the bottom of the dish evenly.

5. Gently transfer the dough to the baking dish, letting one side touch the oil, then gently flip the dough over so the other side is coated in oil. Be sure to handle the dough as little as possible so it doesn't deflate.

6. Cover and let the dough rise at room temperature for about an hour or so until it's soft and jiggly. At this point the dough should almost fill the dish and be very close to the top.

7. Preheat the oven to 475°F. After the dough has risen, lightly coat your fingers in oil. Gently press your fingertips into the dough until they reach the bottom of the pan. This will create dimples. Repeat this process until you've created dimples all over the top of the dough.

8. Drizzle 1 tablespoon of olive oil over the dough, then sprinkle with fresh rosemary and sea salt.

9. Bake on the lower rack of the oven for 15 minutes or until dough surface is brown with a golden color in the dimples.

10. Remove from the oven, then use the parchment to lift the focaccia out of the dish. Transfer to a wire cooling rack to remove the parchment strip.

11. Turn off the oven and place the focaccia back in, directly on the lower rack, for another 5 minutes or until the sides are golden brown and crisp.

12. Remove from the oven again and transfer back to the wire rack to cool completely.

INDEX